Original title:
Purpose Found in the Chaos

Copyright © 2025 Creative Arts Management OÜ
All rights reserved.

Author: Hugo Fitzgerald
ISBN HARDBACK: 978-1-80566-215-0
ISBN PAPERBACK: 978-1-80566-510-6

Unseen Flowers Amongst the Weeds

In a garden of troubles, I tripped on a toad,
Where weeds dance and laugh, I've dropped my load.
Yet in the ruckus, like stars in the night,
A dandelion's wink brings me pure delight.

The squirrels gather nuts, they're plotting a heist,
While I'm lost in the rumbles, I can't find my slice.
But between all the thorns, and spade's heavy clink,
A row of bright daisies make me stop and think.

With mud on my shoes, I embrace the unknown,
Though accident-prone, I'm no longer alone.
Each flower I find, like a joke from the past,
Reminds me to giggle, through chaos I've cast.

Life's a circus, it seems, as I stray off my path,
Where weeds whisper secrets, and laughter is math.
In tangled intentions, I might look askew,
Yet unseen flowers dance, they know just what to do.

Lost and Found in the Shuffle

In the laundry, socks collide,
One's a hero, one's a guide.
T-shirts dance, they jig and twirl,
Lost in the spin of a cotton whirl.

Keys tucked under the couch's nest,
Remote controls become a quest.
Juggling life with mismatched flair,
Finding joy in what's not there.

A Kaleidoscope of Resilience

Life's a puzzle, pieces stray,
Colors clash in a bright ballet.
Laughter bubbles in broken glass,
We wear our failures like a class.

Spilled coffee, a morning art,
Chaos pronounced, yet we take part.
With wobbly steps, we make our way,
Dancing through the disarray.

Navigating the Uncharted Waves

Surfboards wobble on sandy tracks,
Seagulls chuckle, there's no looking back.
Just when you think you've found your beat,
A wave of laughter rises to greet.

Maps are useless in this tide,
But we'll chase what we can't hide.
With a splash and a giggle, we ride the storm,
Making folly a habit, a quirky norm.

Fragments of a Whimsical Journey

Backpacks bursting with odd things,
Fruit snacks, doodles, and rubber bands flings.
Every step's a whimsical chance,
As we stumble through this funny dance.

Grapes become our travel mates,
Discussing life while sealing fates.
With giggles echoing through the night,
Every mishap sparkles bright.

Growing Wild in a Cracked Soil

In the garden of nonsense, weeds take the lead,
With dandelions dancing, they plot and they seed.
The cabbages giggle, in bright silly hats,
While carrots play tag with the lazy old rats.

Sunflowers wink at the clouds passing by,
As bees hire the daisies to sing sweet lullabies.
The soil is all cracked, but we're growing quite tall,
In a jungle of chaos, we're loving it all.

Seraphs in the Chaos

In clouds made of marshmallows, angels take flight,
Winged squeaky toys, oh what a silly sight!
They tumble and giggle, through mayhem they glide,
Sprinkling confetti when chaos goes wide.

With halos of spaghetti, they dance on the breeze,
Twirling through troubles with absolute ease.
They whisper in mischief, spread laughter galore,
Reminding us all that it's fine to be more.

Discovering Paths in the Rough

Lost in the woods with a compass that's broke,
A squirrel is laughing, oh what a joke!
The trees clap their branches, they sway to the beat,
While I trip on my laces, and stumble on feet.

The rocks throw a party, they rattle and roll,
As I search for the path, they take on a stroll.
With every wrong turn, more laughter I find,
Wandering wildly, I'm one of a kind.

Whirling Tides of Time

In the whirlpool of minutes, cast away my clock,
I'll surf on the seconds, ride waves made of rock.
With jellyfish jokes and seaweed to share,
I navigate lovingly through time's wiggly air.

The dolphins are giggling, they know how to play,
They'll teach me to dance on a wild ocean sway.
As tides pull and push, I'll just laugh and dive,
In a sea of confusion, I'm more than alive!

Cacophony of New Beginnings

In the tumble of socks and jangling keys,
A dance of missed steps brings laughter with ease.
Coffee spills - a morning delight,
Life's a circus, oh what a sight!

A cat in a hat on a bicycle rides,
Chasing the chaos with nimble strides.
Everyone's shouting, yet peace can be found,
In the mess, unintentional joy abounds.

Navigating through the Noise

GPS lost, we're now on a spree,
Driving in circles, just you and me.
Turn left at the poodle, right by the cat,
Life's a fun journey, imagine that!

A parade of mishaps, we wave and we grin,
Finding gold in the muck—let the adventure begin!
Glitches galore, and yet we survive,
With laughter as fuel, we truly thrive.

Harmony Amidst Hectic Skies

Umbrella upside down as the raindrops fall,
The air filled with giggles, oh what a brawl!
Dancing squirrels join in the fun,
As we trip over puddles, laughing and run.

Lunch in a frenzy, forks fly through the air,
Bread on the ceiling, we chuckle and share.
In these moments of chaos, we find our sweet beat,
Navigating the madness with light-hearted feet.

Portraits of the Unexpected

A llama in pajamas steals the show,
Posing for selfies, what a way to go!
Unexpected guests, a clown with a pie,
Spattering laughter as we shuffle by.

An artist with talent for doodling chaos,
Turns frowns into smiles, what a nifty path!
Colors collide, yet beauty remains,
In this whirlwind of wonder, joy entertains.

Phoenix Rising from the Ashes

From burnt toast comes the phoenix bright,
An epic tale of morning fright.
With coffee spilled and socks mismatched,
Life's crazy plot, we're all attached.

We trip and tumble, make a mess,
Yet laughter echoes in distress.
Like feathers swirling in the breeze,
We rise again, it's all a tease.

Trials Beneath the Turbulent Sky

A cloudburst falls on picnic day,
Soggy sandwiches in dismay.
We dance in puddles, who needs dry?
With every slip, we laugh and sigh.

Under storms, our smiles gleam,
Strangers join to form a team.
We face the wind with open arms,
While chaos spins its quirky charms.

Mosaic of the Disarrayed

Bricks of chaos form a wall,
Like a toddler's tower, it could fall.
Yet in this mess, a treasure lies,
A wonky art that delights the eyes.

With mismatched pieces, we create,
A portrait of schadenfreude fate.
Each flaw a story, bold and bright,
In the chaos, we find our light.

Truths in the Tangle

A hairbrush caught in a wild nest,
Tangled truths put to the test.
We laugh as we unravel the knots,
Finding paths in all our spots.

Life's a yarn all knotted tight,
A playful dance of wrong and right.
In every twist, a grin appears,
For joy is found among our fears.

Blossoms in the Ruins

Among the rubble, flowers bloom,
Dancing through a dusty room.
Cracks in concrete, nature's cheer,
Who knew chaos could be so dear?

A cat naps on a fallen chair,
While pigeons steal the show from air.
Messy paint splatters speak of thrill,
Life finds a way, against the will.

The laundry hangs from twisted wire,
Each sock a flag, proclaiming desire.
In the clutter, joy is found,
Laughter echoes all around.

Coffee spills on an old blueprint,
As dreams get tangled, still they flit.
A cactus stands on a crooked shelf,
Mocking those who can't laugh at self.

Echoes of a Shattered Dream

A shattered vase, a broken chance,
Confetti from a vanished dance.
In madness, find the giggle there,
Watch as sadness trips on air.

A sock war rages on the floor,
Each pair a tale of missed rapport.
Lopsided chairs and squeaky doors,
Invite you to burst with metaphor.

Lemonade spills on the old guitar,
Notes mix with chaos, a messy bazaar.
Who needs a plan when you can sway?
As laughter leads, we lose our way.

In the rubble, a dog woofs loud,
Chasing dreams that once seemed proud.
Let's toast to the art of blunder,
And find joy in the wild thunder.

In the Heart of Mayhem

Cereal rain on a sunny day,
Milk rivers flowing, come what may.
In the kitchen, chaos reigns,
While giggles dance like sugar canes.

Wobbly towers of grocery bags,
A game of balance with snarky jags.
Who needs order in a fun jet stream?
Just ride the wave of this wild dream.

Spaghetti strings adorn the wall,
Perfect art for those who'd fall.
In every slip and trip, delight,
As laughter erupts in sheer moonlight.

Under tables, echoes tell,
Of messy stories that went so well.
In the heart of the lovely wreck,
We find the joy in each strange speck.

A Canvas of Unruly Colors

The paint splatters tell a tale,
Of brush strokes wild, a grand derail.
One blue cat barks atop a chair,
While laughter drips from the open air.

Doodles dance on the fridge with flair,
An abstract masterpiece everywhere.
The chaos mocks the straight-lined fate,
In quirks, we celebrate the great.

Broken crayons hold fun within,
In each poor choice, a brand new win.
The curtains twist like pirate ships,
Bold colors smile with mischievous lips.

Confetti falls from a ceiling fan,
A rainbow path through the disheveled plan.
With every shade, a jest is spun,
In this wild art, we find the fun.

The Dance of Disarray

In the kitchen, flour flies,
Pasta twists like wild butterflies,
Dishes wobble, forks do prance,
Who knew chaos could lead to a dance?

Cats on countertops, doing their thing,
As I juggle the eggs, they start to sing,
Spaghetti's tangled, I wear a sauce crown,
In this lovely chaos, I won't frown.

Mixing up tunes while I fry the roast,
The dog joins in, thinks he's a host,
With every pot that clinks and clatters,
Chaos unfolds, and laughter scatters.

So here I stand, a chef of delight,
In the midst of the mess, everything's right,
With a pinch of madness, a dash of fun,
In our dance of disarray, we are all one.

From Fractures to Wholeness

I tripped on a sock, then fell on the rug,
Landed on Legos, oh what a snug,
The dog licked my face, said, 'Hey, no harm!'
In this silly tumble, I found some charm.

Gathering fragments, a puzzle's all jumbled,
Yet in the chaos, my laughter is fumbled,
Toys in the air, a rainbow of mess,
Who knew fractured fun could be such a bless?

Dust bunnies dance as I sweep them alight,
The cat gives a flick, makes everything right,
In a world upside down, with giggles and cheer,
These broken things bring our joy ever near.

So let's connect our quirks, embrace every flaw,
In a whirlwind of laughter, the love is the law,
From scattered little bits, we create our whole,
In this mad little game, we reach for our soul.

Finding Stars in the Storm

Raindrops carpet the roof with a thud,
I bartered my plans for a pot full of mud,
Umbrellas flip and folks shout 'Oh no!'
Yet in this wet dance, watch bright spirits glow!

Traffic jams play their honking refrain,
While coffee spills, art from strain,
But under the cloud, we splash like kids,
In puddles of laughter, forget our grids.

Lightning strikes with a zany hue,
As we dodge and weave, pretend we're new,
Through torrents and giggles, we forge our light,
Finding our stars, even in stormy night.

So raise up your voice, sing loud in the rain,
For in every storm, there's a wild, sweet gain,
With friends at our sides, let chaos take flight,
We'll find all the stars that shimmer in plight.

The Quiet in the Maelstrom

In the heart of the whirlwind, I sip my tea,
While laundry explodes, no sign of debris,
Kids dance with wild hair, laughter like bells,
And I'm at the center, where calmness dwells.

The dog chases chaos, it's quite entertaining,
As I dodge flying toys, my sanity waning,
Yet in this mad maze, it feels just like play,
Finding a joke in the mess of the day.

Ice cream on faces, a colorful sight,
Amidst the pandemonium, everything's right,
A symphony of noise, but I catch the tune,
In the ruggedest moments, we're over the moon.

So embrace the maelstrom, don't turn the page,
For in this wild laughter, we're all center stage,
In quiet within chaos, like candy in stew,
The sweet little moments make life bright and true.

Embracing the Unraveled Threads

In a world where socks just vanish,
My laundry has a strange new plan.
Two shoes, one sole, quite the banish,
Yet I still make it, oh yes I can!

Lipstick's on the cat, so sly,
The dog wears my favorite hat.
In the chaos, I just sigh,
And dance with a chicken, imagine that!

Coffee spills on my best shirt,
But life's a splash of crazy fun.
I've tripped on air and hit the dirt,
Each stumble an unplanned run!

With mismatched plates and glasses too,
I raise a toast to silly nights.
For all the mess, I'll say it's true,
It's laughter that gives life its heights!

Serenity in the Shattered Pieces

My breakfast broke and flew away,
Eggs decided to play hide and seek.
Toast was steadfast, came what may,
But the jam just found the dog's cheek!

A puzzle piece stuck in my shoe,
Every step feels like a fight.
Yet what's that smell? Oh, it's the stew!
Dinner's chaos brings pure delight!

As I trip on my cat's loud snore,
I question what I'm working for.
Yet with every tumble to the floor,
A giggle sparks, makes me want more!

Amid the wrecks and random sighs,
I find the joy in each mishap.
For every mess, laughter replies,
In this circus, I take my lap!

When Rain Falls on the Fractured

Raindrops dance on my window sill,
While I find my shoes in the fridge.
A soggy sock? What a thrill!
Life's strange mix, a topsy bridge!

The kettle whistles, oh dear me,
I've brewed a soup that smells like sweat.
In puddles, my toes feel so free,
A whimsical day without regret!

Umbrellas fly like kites in flight,
As I dodge splashes from the street.
The chaos makes my day so bright,
With wet socks, I still tap my feet!

So here I stand, drenched to the bone,
Giggling madly, life's sweet pain.
In every storm, I've always known,
The laughter makes me dance again!

The Beauty of Tornadoes' Dance

My hair's a mess, it takes the prize,
A whirlwind of life all in a swirl.
With bananas flying through the skies,
I laugh as my sanity starts to twirl!

The blender's broken, oh what fun,
It splattered soup across the room.
Yet in the chaos, I have won,
A masterpiece in every bloom!

With cupcakes tumbling from the shelf,
And icing splats on my cat's nose,
I smile wide, not caring for self,
In this madness, my joy grows!

So let the twisters whirl and spin,
A joyful chaos is the key.
In the dance of wild, I dive in,
Embracing the storm, I feel so free!

The Search Beneath the Surface

In the ocean's depths, I dove,
Where seaweed danced and fish rove.
I lost my keys, my lunch, my shoe,
But found a crab who sang a tune!

With bubbles popping all around,
I followed a fish, then got stuck, profound.
He swam away with a cheeky wink,
While I pondered snacking on a pink drink!

The currents pulled me here and there,
Trying to ride a wave, I fell unaware.
But lo and behold, in all that splash,
I found my sense of humor, what a clash!

So here's to chaos, with laughter loud,
Where lost things join the ocean crowd.
In watery chaos, my joy ignites,
I'll find the funny in all my plights!

Stormy Winds and Starlit Skies

Up in the sky, the storm did brew,
I donned my cape, out I flew!
The winds howled loud, my hat took flight,
Chasing it down felt quite a sight!

Lightning crackled like a show in town,
I lost my way but wore a frown.
Found a cloud that brewed some tea,
"Just sit awhile and laugh with me!"

Raindrops taped a tune on my head,
I danced in puddles, who needs a bed?
With stars peeking through the raucous night,
I twirled and twirled, oh what a plight!

So let the storms come, loud and proud,
I'll juggle umbrellas, sing, and crowd.
In chaos I'll find each silly laugh,
Under starlit skies, take my goofy path!

Secrets within the Scattered Stars

I looked up high, stars all a-twinkle,
Found a comet with a giant sprinkle.
He said, "Hey pal! Want a ride?"
But I fell off, oh what a glide!

Down through the darkness, I did plummet,
A meteor's tail? Nope, just my stomach.
Rolling through space like a silly fool,
I landed on the Moon's cool stool!

Met a space cat with glowing eyes,
He whispered secrets, drowned in lies.
"Follow your nose to the milky way,
Where cheese awaits, come here and play!"

So here I am, just floating like fluff,
Finding joy in chaos, who needs tough?
With cosmic giggles filling the void,
In scattered stars, I'm the one enjoyed!

Finding the Glitter in Grit

In a muddy patch, I tripped and fell,
Covered in dirt, I turned to yell.
But as I stood, my eyes shone bright,
For glitter lay hidden, what a sight!

A pig strolled by with a sparkly tail,
I chuckled at such a strange detail.
"Join the party," it squeaked with cheer,
"We all have dirt but shine's so near!"

With feathers, stones, and a real bad hat,
Life's full of mess, all covered in chat.
Scrub away the world's grimy grit,
You'll find a sparkle if you just commit!

Through muck and laughter, I will roam,
In my glittery mess, I feel at home.
From chaos blooms the wildest bliss,
In every stumble, there's joy, I insist!

Whispers Amidst the Turbulence

In the storm of socks and scattered shoes,
I swear the cat has picked her muse.
Twirling spoons on the kitchen floor,
A dance so funny, who could ask for more?

Juggling life like a clown in a ring,
Oops, there goes my morning zing.
Coffee spills in a gravity-defying spree,
At least the floor gets a taste of me!

Chasing dreams on a bumpy ride,
A flat tire? Nah, my joy's the guide.
Bathing in laughter that spills and splashes,
Finding gold where the chaos crashes.

So here I stand, a joyful mess,
Kites and papers in a breezy dress.
Every twist leads to laughter's path,
Finding the fun in the aftermath!

Fragments of Clarity

Caught between the crumbs and crumbs,
I search for sense in the pops and hums.
A lost remote controls my fate,
Maybe it's hiding with the missing mate.

Spaghetti twirls like a ballerina's spin,
Tomato sauce? Well, let the war begin!
Dishes stacked in a leaning tower,
A mountain of chaos gives me power.

Puppies chase their own wagging tails,
Each flop and stumble? Epic trails.
Bubbles burst with a gleeful pop,
In this mad chaos, I can't stop!

Sailing boats made of paper planes,
Riding the waves of silly gains.
Fragments found in the wildest spree,
Who knew that chaos could tickle me?

Symphony of the Unraveled

A symphony starts with a squeaky wheel,
Tickle me pink, that's the ideal feel.
Confetti storms from the ceiling fan,
A party on high—oh, this was the plan!

Clumsy moves on the dancing floor,
With every misstep, I explore more.
Laughing notes in a jumbled tune,
The orchestra's chaos makes me swoon.

Dishes crash like cymbals in play,
And the cat just sits back and says 'Nay!'
Yet here we are, in this mad parade,
Finding the fun in the misfit charade.

Every note's a twist of delight,
Even when dinner's a cooking fright.
Bring on the chaos, let laughter reign,
In this wild concert, there's nothing to feign!

The Kaleidoscope of Meaning

Colors swirl in a dizzying show,
Each spin reveals what I didn't know.
Rainbows clash in a playful duel,
Finding sense in the absurd rule.

Cupcakes fly like ideas on wings,
As frosting splats, my mind just sings.
Wobbling jars of jam and cheer,
I've stumbled right into the wild frontier.

Tickle my fancies with silly pranks,
In this swirl, I shall raise my thanks.
Worlds collide in a dance divine,
A kaleidoscope sparkles, how truly fine!

So here's to chaos, my merry friend,
Each twist and turn, a joyful blend.
In laughter's embrace, I now reside,
With meaning that's silly, wide-open, and wide!

Harmony in the Havoc

In a kitchen where dishes collide,
Pasta tangoing with cat food side by side.
The cat gives a wink, as if to say,
"Life's a party, but I'm just here to play!"

The laundry may swirl like a twirling dervish,
Colors clash, but who could ever nourish
A world of bland, when chaos is grand?
The missing sock is just part of the band!

From Entropy Comes Creation

In a world where things tumble and fall,
A new sculpture forms from the cluttered sprawl.
Sticky notes blossom like flowers in spring,
Who knew that chaos could give birth to bling?

The blender explodes, oh what a thrill!
Smoothie confetti, a sticky sweet spill.
One peach, two bananas, and a curious shoe,
Gives us breakfast, and a laugh or two!

Serendipity in the Storm

Umbrellas flip unexpectedly high,
As raindrops dance, they giggle and sigh.
The weather forecast said to stay dry,
But puddle jumping is worth a good try!

In the midst of the wild and woeful rain,
I found my lost shoe, now that's a gain!
A dance with the wind, my hat takes flight,
Who knew a storm could be such delight?

Threads of Meaning in Madness

Knots in the yarn, as I knit through the day,
Each twist a reminder, come what may.
A scarf with odd colors, bright wild and bold,
A masterpiece born from a box of old gold.

Crayon scribbles cover the living room floor,
A map to adventure, oh what's in store?
Every scribble a story, no need to ask,
In this canvas of chaos, let's dive in—what a blast!

The Mosaic of Lost Directions

In the jumble of my thoughts, I roam,
Lost my keys, and I can't find home.
Directions scribbled on a napkin thin,
I guess I'll just follow where the cats have been.

Wandered into a dance class by mistake,
Twinkle toes ranging from a jello shake,
With every step, I trip and spin,
Who knew chaos held a little fun within?

Maps are ludicrous, they lead to nowhere,
So I scribble my own, who needs the air?
With each wrong turn, I find a new face,
In this mayhem, I've found a happy place.

Life's a puzzle with pieces misplaced,
But in each corner, laughter is traced.
And if you squint, it all makes sense,
Dancing streets become my current suspense.

Glimmers of Truth Beneath the Waves

The ocean's waves are wild and loud,
Frolicking with fish, I'm lost in the crowd.
Sand in my shorts, a comedy act,
Searching for shells but finding a crack.

The seagulls caw, they steal my fries,
An acrobatic heist right before my eyes.
A splash of salt, an unexpected swim,
Diving for truth, I'm just winging it, slim.

I ride the waves on a noodle bright,
Bobbing along in sheer delight.
With every dive, I laugh out my fears,
Funny how chaos becomes my cool cheers.

Crashing waves, yet I still float by,
In tangled thoughts, I learn to fly.
The tide pulls me, but I find my groove,
In splashes of chaos, I make my move.

Resilience in the Riptide

Caught in a riptide, what a delight,
Pull me to surfboards that take to flight.
Flailing and wailing, I surf on a dream,
What a mad wave, or so it would seem.

I smile at strangers floating with flair,
We're all just bobbing, glib without care.
"Grab my hand!" I shout, making friends on the way,
Laughing at life, come what may.

Each wave is a riddle wrapped in a curl,
Chaos my partner as I spin and whirl.
Saltwater laughter, quite the best blend,
Riptides may twist, but I won't let them bend.

So ride the wave to the whimsical shore,
Where chaos cheerfully opens each door.
In the foam and spray, we find our bliss,
When life's a wild ride, you can't help but kiss.

Sifting through Shadows

In the corner lurks the whoopee cushion,
Shadows whisper secrets, causing a commotion.
I giggle at mysteries, peeking around,
Finding joy in the things that astound.

The clock ticks backward, or is it just me?
Sifting through moments, unexpectedly free.
Laughter echoes through shadowy sights,
Where every giggle could turn into flights.

I chase my own tail, a dog in disguise,
Finding trouble in the blink of my eyes.
In a world of fickle, I'm fully awake,
Bumbling through shadows, catching a break.

So here's to the farcical, the strange and the fun,
In every shadow, there's hiding a pun.
With each little quirk, I prance and I sway,
In this silly chaos, I'm happy to stay.

Beauty from Brokenness

In a world that's quite askew,
I tripped on my way to brew.
But the coffee spilled, a glorious sight,
It brewed a pattern, oh what a delight!

My socks don't match, they dance with glee,
A fashion statement, wouldn't you agree?
They laughed as I stumbled on my way,
In chaos, bright joy seemed to play!

Each crack in the wall tells a tale,
Of how I fell and tried to prevail.
Laughter echoes, my heart sets free,
In every misstep, I find me!

So here's to the mess, the laughter, the fun,
In wacky designs, my spirit has run.
For brokenness sings a curious tune,
And I waltz with the stars, under the moon!

Navigating the Storm's Heart

Raindrops tap dance on my hat,
Each one a surprising acrobat.
I spin like a top in torrential rain,
While umbrellas flip, oh what a gain!

Lightning winks, as thunder chimes,
In this wild weather, I try new rhymes.
A sailboat's my hat, I'm ready to drift,
Navigating life's chaotic shift!

The winds throw confetti, I'll take a chance,
Dancing in puddles, come join the dance!
With each gust, my worries scatter away,
In stormy chaos, I find a way!

So let the clouds rumble, let the sky roar,
I'll find the best inside the uproar.
In the heart of chaos, I'm not alone,
I laugh with the thunder, I've found my tone!

Order in Colorful Confusion

A rainbow spilled on my living room floor,
Socks and shoes shoestrung, what's in store?
My cat wears a hat, looking sublime,
In this colorful mess, we dance in rhyme!

Paint pots topple, splattering cheer,
Each color a giggle, let's draw it near.
I trip over brushes, but giggles ensue,
In confusion's embrace, I start anew!

My jumbled closet, a puzzle at best,
Finding my shirt's like a fun treasure quest.
Amidst all the chaos, bright laughter grows,
In each little mix, a new life glows!

So here's to the mismatched, the quirky, and wild,
In chaos, I'm ever the curious child.
With crayons and giggles, let the fuss unfold,
In colorful chaos, new stories are told!

The Alchemy of Uncertainty

In a pot of confusion, I stir with a grin,
Who knows what magic is waiting within?
A sprinkle of laughter, a dash of surprise,
From chaos emerges where humor lies.

Every misstep is like a new spell,
Transforming each flop into something swell.
I've juggled spaghetti and fallen on cheese,
In life's foolish kitchen, I find my ease!

The recipe's written in laughter and fun,
With each little blunder, I savor that run.
Burnt toast turns to croissants in the heat,
With a pinch of uncertainty, life's quite a treat!

So let the world spin, let the pots clatter,
In the chaos, there's joy; that's the matter.
With each tasty flub, my spirit takes flight,
In this alchemy game, I'm the star of the night!

Embracing the Whirl

In a dance of socks that don't quite match,
I twirl in circles, feeling quite the catch.
Chaos giggles as I trip and spin,
Each tumble a treasure, let the fun begin!

Coffee spills on my lap, a playful splash,
The dog runs by, in a frantic dash.
I chase him down, what a splendid sight,
We're crafting joy in this funny plight!

Bills are flying, like leaves in the air,
My inbox buzzes, I'm caught in the snare.
I'll wear my cape, let the madness reel,
In this circus of life, I'm the jester who feels!

So here's to the mayhem, the gleeful chase,
Where every wild twist leads to a happy place.
Chaos may reign, but I'll always cheer,
For in the whirlwind, I find my clear steer!

Through Clarity in Turmoil

The blender roars like a lion with glee,
As I juggle spaghetti and cups of sweet tea.
Pasta on the ceiling, oh what a treat,
Who knew dinner could turn into a beat?

In the kitchen chaos, I'm a star on a stage,
Learning the dance moves of culinary rage.
With flour clouds thickening, I bow and I twirl,
Even when burnt, I still give it a whirl!

The dog's in the mix, mixing up my mind,
Thought bubbles burst while you're slow-footed blind.
He steals my snack, then races away,
Life's a comedy, come laugh, come play!

Amidst the clamor, there shines a bright glow,
New ideas sprout like a garden in flow.
With giggles and grumbles, we find our escape,
In this beautiful mess, we find our own shape!

Whispers in the Whirlwind

Winds howling louder, I grab my hat tight,
My umbrella flips, oh what a sight!
I'm a kite in the storm, caught in a freeze,
Dancing with raindrops as they float with ease.

Cats chase their tails, dogs leap in delight,
Atop of my roof (what a feline flight!).
In the midst of a whirlwind, I laugh at the rain,
Finding joy in each splash, joy from the pain.

My pants have a tear that's a style revolution,
As I catwalk in puddles, a fashion solution!
Twisting and twirling, I grab life's stray chance,
In chaos and laughter, we weave a fine dance.

So let the skies rumble and thunder Paul's tune,
I'll spin in the cyclone, I'll waltz with the moon.
With whispers of madness, we'll craft a fine tale,
A melody sung while we laugh through the gale!

A Symphony Amidst the Storm

Raindrops are drummers, tapping away,
While thunder claps out a wild ballet.
Nature's symphony plays with a twist,
Each note is a giggle that can't be missed.

In muddy puddles, we leap and we bound,
A splash here and there, laughter all around.
With umbrellas upside down, we're quite the sight,
In this orchestra of chaos, we dance through the night.

The cat caught the mouse, then slipped on the mat,
We chuckle and roar, "Look at that!"
In this humorous mayhem, we all play our part,
Finding harmony woven with chaos at heart.

So let the storm rage, let it howl and let loose,
We'll conduct our symphony, pouring joy like a juice.
With every wild note, we create and inspire,
In the midst of the tempest, our spirits will fire!

Jigsaw of the Spirited

Pieces scattered all around,
A puzzle speaks without a sound.
If life's a game of beat the clock,
   I'd rather use a rubber rock.

A corner here, a border there,
   Finding joy in my own despair.
Why fit in when you can stand out?
Chaos makes me want to shout!

So grab a drink and take a seat,
   Life's a dance, not a repeat.
With mismatched socks and crumpled hats,
   I'll weave the weirdness, just like cats.

In this jigsaw, laughter's key,
   Crazy pieces fit with glee.
So when life's wild, just hold on tight,
   Our vivid chaos feels so right.

Blazing Trails in Chaos

Hiking through the tangled weeds,
I'm the captain of wild misdeeds.
Every twist and turn I take,
Might end in some giant quake.

With a map that looks like cheese,
I'll stumble, laugh, and dodge the bees.
GPS? Nah, I prefer the mess,
Who needs calm when chaos is best?

Each misstep is a dance so grand,
With every fall, I take a stand.
In the woods where squirrels wear hats,
I find my way with wobbly chats.

So let the trails be lost and wild,
In this madness, I'm a child.
A blazing trail of giggles sown,
Where chaos reigns, I'm never alone.

Embracing the Unexpected Serenade

With marching bands in silly hats,
I serenade the dancing cats.
The unexpected tunes that flow,
Make every moment steal the show.

A duck in shoes leads the parade,
While laughter's currency is made.
Confetti bursts from every door,
Life's a stage and I want more!

As guitars strum on flying chairs,
And prancing llamas start their fairs,
I'll twirl and spin in pure delight,
Singing melodies of the night.

So let's embrace the quirky show,
In chaos blooms the finest flow.
Together we'll dance, sing, and sway,
In this unexpected cabaret.

Color in the Wild Whirl

Spinning tops in shades so bright,
Colors whirl within the night.
A canvas splattered, wild and free,
Who knew chaos could be so zany?

With purple parrots leading parades,
And jellybeans that dodge their raids,
I toss my brush with all my might,
Creating laughter, pure delight.

In a swirl where rubber ducks play,
Life's a circus, come what may.
Let balloons float wherever they wish,
In this whirl, let's paint our dish.

So grab your colors, make a mess,
In vibrant chaos, feel the zest.
With giggles bursting from every swirl,
Life's a masterpiece in a wild whirl.

Light in the Eye of the Cyclone

In the storm's eye, we twirl and spin,
With umbrellas upside down, let the fun begin.
Raindrops like marbles, we leap and glide,
Finding laughter where chaos tried to hide.

Tornadoes dance with a whirling laugh,
While squirrels play chess on a broken path.
Lost in the whirlwind, we trip and play,
Who knew a cyclone could brighten the day?

As shirts fly flat like superheroes' capes,
We break into song, like a choir of apes.
The thunder's a drummer, we all join in,
Making sweet symphonies in the madness din.

So if you find yourself caught in a breeze,
Surrender to joy, let your worries freeze.
In the cyclone's embrace, we swirl like confetti,
With every gust, finding joy, ever ready.

The Art of Finding Clarity

In the clutter of life, I trip on my toes,
Juggling my thoughts like a circus dose.
With coffee in hand and a pancake hat,
I'll figure it out while I'm busy like that.

The chaos unfolds like a comic book page,
Wormholes of nonsense, I'm center stage.
While socks and keys play hide and seek,
I'll laugh at the mess, finding answers unique.

Words spill like jelly from a tipped-over jar,
I sift through the gooey, I'm a purpose bazaar.
Each mishap a clue in this riddle of mine,
Clarity dances, though it's hard to define.

With a wink and a nod, let's embrace the strife,
Finding meaning in madness, the art of our life.
So grab your paintbrush and color outside,
For clarity thrives where quirky things abide.

Dancing Through the Tempest

With a hat made of fish and boots made of cheese,
I'm dancing through storms like a cat in the breeze.
Lightning claps hands, the thunder's our beat,
In this silly soiree, watch us twirl on our feet.

Raindrops are marbles, I giggle and slip,
Each puddle a bounce, join in on the trip.
The chaos concocts a delightful charade,
As we waltz on the winds that the tempest has made.

With a shimmy and shake, we spin like a top,
A carousel circus where laughter won't stop.
Twirling through gusts, we chuckle and chow,
Finding humor in wildness, the here and the now.

So grab a wild partner from the storm's swirling croon,
We'll salsa with chaos under a tempestuous moon.
In every wild whirl, our happiness grows,
Dancing through tempests where true joy flows.

Chaos Unveils the Hidden

In the mess of my room, there's a treasure or two,
Like socks with a secret and crumbs made for stew.
Between towering laundry and dust bunnies wide,
Lies a trove of good giggles, my stash of pride.

Unearthed in jars labeled 'maybe' and 'whoops',
I find my lost sanity in yesterday's scoops.
From tangled-up wires to a duck-shaped lamp,
I chuckle aloud, feeling like a champ.

The chaos surrounds, but it's not all askew,
For hidden in clutter, there's magic in view.
Each mishap a story, each blunder a clue,
A symphony rising, of life fresh and new.

So here's to the mess, to the scattered delight,
For chaos reveals what's been hiding in sight.
With a wink, I'll embrace what the wildness has shown,
In the jumble and jive, I find my own throne.

Revelations in the Ruin

In the rubble, a squirrel pranced,
Life continues, the world danced.
Amidst the chaos, I lost my keys,
But found a cat who made me sneeze.

The toaster laughed, it burned my bread,
While the blender sang, I danced instead.
In every crack, a secret laid,
Like a sock puppet parade, unafraid.

A shoe flew past, it had a grin,
Captured in mayhem, the real fun begins.
With penguins wearing hats, a sight to behold,
In this wild mess, stories unfold.

A Map in the Madness

A crumpled map said, "Go right here!"
Yet I tripped on my shoelace, oh dear!
Every twist turned out upside down,
The compass spun, laughed like a clown.

I sought my fortune in a candy shop,
But ended with pickles, it made me hop.
In this swirl of flavor, a giggle was found,
A rainbow of chaos above and around.

My GPS yelled, "Recalculating now!"
As I danced with llamas in a purple cow.
Through confusion and twists, through bends and curves
I found delight in all the swerves.

Serenity Amongst the Whirlwind

As leaves twirl round in a frolicsome spree,
A squirrel dodged rain, then slipped on a pea.
With umbrellas dancing like they're on fire,
All soaked in laughter, our spirits aspire.

The wind howled loud, like a mad old friend,
And ice cream cones began to blend.
A parade of ducks in floats made of bread,
Riding the current with giggles instead.

In whirlwinds of chaos, humor is king,
As a dog wore spectacles, oh what a thing!
Through slapstick mishaps, we twirl and spin,
In the eye of the storm, that's where we begin.

Harmony in Fractured Notes

Off-key songs played on a rusty flute,
A cat with a tambourine wanted to hoot.
Jellybeans spilled on a dance floor of mud,
While I tried to waltz, I just made a dud.

The music of chaos, a sweet serenade,
As I tripped and slid, my dignity betrayed.
Yet laughter erupted, a joyous crescendo,
In fractures and errors, the fun started to show.

A frog jumped high, croaking with flair,
While I tried to join in, lost my balance in air.
With rhythm unhinged and giggles in tow,
We found harmony where the wild breezes blow.

Light Shattered by Shadows

In a room full of socks, odd and mismatched,
I discovered a treasure—my mind was hatched.
The cat in the corner, plotting a snack,
Had more wisdom than me—there's no turning back.

Jelly beans spilled on the floor like confetti,
Each one a reminder, life can be petty.
A dance with the dust bunnies, swirling around,
In this circus of chaos, joy can be found.

My coffee went flying, a latte ballet,
It landed on papers—oh, what a display!
But amid all the spills and the sounds of a crash,
I laughed at the chaos, a riotous splash.

So here's to the laughter when life goes awry,
Like a giraffe in a tutu, reaching for the sky.
In the whirlwind of madness, let whimsy ignite,
And dance with the shadows till day turns to night.

Finding Your Way in Broken Glass

Stumbling through life like a clumsy old bear,
With shards of my dreams sending sparkles in air.
Each cut and each bruise, part of the show,
I pirouette freely; just watch me go!

A jigsaw of moments, all poking and prying,
Each piece is wacky, it's hard not to be trying.
With laughter as glue, we'll rebuild our glass world,
And make it a masterpiece—watch it unfurl!

My GPS cracked, said, 'Turn left at the glue.'
I laughed at the map, now I know what to do!
In a maze of confusion, I found a funny path,
With giggles and puzzles, I danced up my math.

So here's to the bumps, the jagged little bends,
With humor my friend, and laughter my trends.
In this quirky adventure, I'll sparkle and shine,
Navigating the chaos, oh what a good time!

Landscapes of Uncertainty

Painting with crayons in shades of pure doubt,
Each squiggle and wiggle a laughing shout-out.
A map made of pizza, who said it was wrong?
I'm cruising through chaos; let's sing a loud song!

Clouds like cotton candy float through my mind,
As I waltz through the fields where confusion is kind.
I tripped on a daisy, laughed 'til I cried,
In the landscapes of chaos, I'll joyfully glide.

My compass is broken, but hey, that's just fine,
I'll follow the squirrels—they know how to dine.
Through fogs of absurdity, I'll find my own way,
With giggles and grins, turning night into day!

In gardens of riddle, where nonsense takes hold,
I'll gather the giggles, be brave and be bold.
Each twist in my journey, a tale to unfold,
In this wild, wacky world, let the laughter be told!

The Gift of Turbulent Days

Woke up in a whirlwind, my hair is a fright,
Had cereal for dinner, now isn't that bright?
In the chaos of mornings, a dance with a sock,
I found hidden treasures—like gold on the clock.

Chipmunk in a tie, giving me a speech,
About embracing the chaos, what a wild reach!
It's not the straight roads but the bumps in the way,
That lead us to laughter, let's dance and let sway!

Rain fell like confetti while I hopped on my bike,
Circuitous routes turning into a hike.
With puddles like mirrors reflecting delight,
I splashed through the madness, oh, what a sight!

So here's to the mayhem that always ensues,
A gift wrapped in chaos—in sparkles and blues.
Let's toast with our coffee, now spilled on the floor,
For in these turbulent days, we find so much more!

Triumph in the Tangled Roots

In the garden of mess, I found my shoe,
A treasure once lost, now covered in goo.
Weeds dance around, in a waltz quite absurd,
Who knew chaos could sing like a mad little bird?

The rake is my ally, we battle as friends,
With each swipe, we giggle, this chaos transcends.
Sprouts of confusion begin to take flight,
In this whirlwind of joy, I take pure delight.

Flip-flops and hedge clippers join in the fray,
With laughter and soil, we savor the day.
Turn over a trowel, embrace all the mess,
Here in the tangle, I've learned to impress.

Triumphant I stand, dirt smudged on my cheek,
The chaos has turned into havens unique.
So here's to the roots, all twisted but bright,
In the wild dance of nature, I've found my delight!

Reflections in the Broken Mirror

A shard of myself stares back from the floor,
With a wink and a grin: "Hey, you need some more!"
Cracks tell the tales of my wild escapade,
In this jigsaw of life, humor's lovingly laid.

Warped are my thoughts, but who's keeping score?
With a laugh in the silence, I open the door.
The fragments of failure, they shimmer and gleam,
In shiny confusion, I'm living the dream.

I host a soirée for the chaos around,
With snacks made of giggles and laughter abound.
Each piece tells a story, each cut shows the fight,
In the wreckage, I find that my heart feels so bright.

So bring on the chaos, I'll dance in the shards,
With characters wild, and some circus-like yards.
In every reflection, I see something new,
In the bonkers embrace, I've rediscovered my true!

The Bright Side of Disarray

Garbage piled high, but I stumble on gold,
This mess is my canvas, with stories untold.
A sock on the ceiling, a cat in the pot,
In this hilarious mess, happiness is caught.

Dust bunnies parade, throwing wild fancy balls,
While the dishes play tag, crashing down from the walls.
The chaos is music, a symphonic delight,
In the flip-flops of life, I'm dancing tonight.

Maps of confusion, I navigate well,
Each route full of laughter, oh, what a spell!
With a pie in the face and crumbs on my nose,
I giggle at all of the chaos that grows.

So here's to the jumbles, the flops, and the spills,
A toast to the wild where absurdity thrills.
In the bright side of chaos, let's all take a ride,
With humor and joy, there's nothing to hide!

Melodies from the Mayhem

In the heart of the clutter, a tune starts to hum,
With a tap of my foot, I welcome the fun.
The blender is singing, while the dog joins the beat,
In this messy concert, oh, what a treat!

Chairs stacked like towers, a fort made of fluff,
Cushions fly high; I'm daring enough!
The rhythm of chaos, a dance so bizarre,
We groove through the clutter, shining like stars.

There's music in chaos, a symphony grand,
With spoons as my batons, just wave your hand.
Melodies mingling with laughter and cheer,
Mayhem's our band, and the ticket is clear.

So gather your friends, let's celebrate loud,
In the jingle of chaos, let's dance with the crowd.
For in every mishap, we find joy anew,
In the melodies played, happiness ensues!

Threads Woven in Disarray

In the tangled yarn of life we weave,
Cats often nap and believe!
Mismatched socks are the latest craze,
Dancing feet in a baffled phase.

Lopsided hats tell tales of woe,
Confetti fights with the wind's wild blow.
Yet in this mess, a quirk emerges,
As laughter in chaos freely surges.

Jumbled plans and broken clocks,
A parade of play where no one mocks.
We trip over dreams like shoes untied,
Finding joy where confusion resides.

So let the pandemonium reign,
In the silliest moments, joy we gain.
For the world's a circus, and we're the show,
In tangled threads, love will grow.

Light Beneath the Tempest

Clouds burst open, rain starts to fall,
Umbrellas flip like a wild brawl.
We splash in puddles, giggling loud,
Finding refuge beneath the cloud.

A seagull swoops, stealing our fries,
As we dodge raindrops and laugh with sighs.
Chaos reigns but we're soaked with glee,
Chasing rainbows is our decree!

Footprints wash away, but smiles remain,
In this soggy dance, no need for a chain.
Slippers squelch, but our spirits soar,
Beneath stormy skies, we crave for more.

So let it rain, let the thunder roll,
With lemonade smiles, we regain control.
In this tempest, we twirl and spin,
Finding light in the chaos, grins within.

Dancing with the Dissonance

A melody plays, yet no one can hear,
Off-beat dancing, but we have no fear.
Tangled limbs in a rhythm so wrong,
We sing with gusto, off key but strong.

Funky shoes and hats askew,
Bumping to the beat that's totally askew.
Chairs become partners, the floor's a stage,
Each twirl and leap, we gain more age.

Party hats may all fall down,
But joy's not lost; it's wearing a crown.
In every clash, there's magic to find,
As we dance with the chaos, joy intertwined.

So let the music play loud and free,
For in this mayhem, we truly agree.
With laughter and love, we twirl and sway,
In dissonance, together we play.

Echoes of Serendipity

Stumbling upon a stray puppy's charm,
Finding delight in a kitchen alarm.
Dropped spaghetti leads to a feast,
As unexpected guests become the least.

An offhand joke leads to contagious grins,
When spilled coffee becomes comic sins.
A humor that dances like socks in the air,
We laugh through mishaps, without a care.

Chasing lost keys, we trip on the floor,
A clatter of laughter that opens the door.
In every blunder, a story unfolds,
As echoes of serendipity mold.

So raise a toast to the little twists,
To moments of chaos and joy that persists.
For life's perfect mess is the sweetest spree,
In mishaps together, we find the key.

Life's Dance in the Disorder

In a world where socks go missing,
I shuffle left, then take a spin.
The dog is barking, neighbor's hissing,
Yet here I am, caught in my grin.

The fridge is bare, I've lost my keys,
My lunch is swimming, maybe a breeze?
I dance with chaos, charmed with ease,
Not all is perfect, but life can tease.

The cat is plotting, eyes narrow and sly,
As I broadcast my thoughts to the sky.
With every misstep, I dare to fly,
In a waltz of wackiness, I can't deny.

Sprinklers launch, a surprise on parade,
I slip and slide, just a little charade.
Laughter erupts, the morning is made,
In this topsy-turvy masquerade.

Beyond the Clamor of Confusion

The coffee's cold, the toast has burned,
Amidst the chaos, I've truly learned.
Whistles and beeps, oh how they churn,
Even in frenzy, joy is returned.

My schedule's a puzzle, pieces wonky and strange,
But laughter escapes through all of the change.
With each little twist, I embrace the derange,
Life's like a sitcom, funny and strange.

Lost in a maze, I take the wrong turn,
Neighbors all gossip, their feathers now churn.
With each little mishap, bright joy I earn,
As life dances on, it's a lesson we learn.

Balancing chaos, the highs and the lows,
I wiggle and waffle, my goofy side shows.
In the midst of the noise, a silly wind blows,
Finding my rhythm, wherever it goes.

In the Wake of the Unraveled

My plans are like yarn in a cat's playful claws,
  Tangled and twisted, leaving me in awe.
  Chasing the chaos, I'm often paused,
 With giggles and grumbles, this is my law.

  The laundry's a mess, oh what a delight,
   I find a sock party in the moonlight.
  Amidst the upheaval, everything's bright,
  With a wink at the chaos, it'll be alright.

Confetti's in the air from last night's success,
As I step on the remnants of unmeasured stress.
 Life tosses surprises, but I feel so blessed,
  In the wake of what's lost, I find my jest.

  With a chuckle, I sift through the fray,
  There's wisdom in chaos, or so I say.
  Dancing with mayhem, I pleasantly sway,
 In this whirl of disorder, I'm here to play.

Hope Speaks in Dissonance

In the jumble of life, I find my tune,
The blender droned on, a loud festive tune.
Eggs scrambled flying, a breakfast monsoon,
Yet laughter rings out beneath the bright moon.

Lost in a chatter of cats and of clamor,
I'm piecing together this wild morning glamour.
With every mishap, I rise and I stammer,
Chaos brings joy that makes my heart hammer.

A coffee spill here, a pancake that flies,
I dodge and I weave, oh the fun never dies.
In the ruckus I grin, as the world spins and sighs,
In the orchestra of life, I'm the one who applies.

So here's to the mayhem, the absolutely mad,
When life gives confusion, I always feel glad.
In the symphony of nonsense, I'm never quite sad,
For hope sings out loud, and I dance with my dad.

Echoes from the Torn Pages

Amidst the fray, I lost my pen,
My notes a mess, where do I begin?
A shopping list turned deep philosophy,
Must I return to grocery remedy?

Chaos reigns, my cat's on the desk,
Knocking over coffee, it's quite grotesque.
I scribble madly, my words in flight,
While socks and keys have joined the fight.

Between the laughter and the cries,
A sandwich flies, it hits the skies.
A dance of chaos, oh what a sight,
I find my muse in this absurd plight.

So here I stand, in this cluttered space,
Finding joy in the wild embrace.
For in the chaos, life's jokes unite,
Turning blunders into sheer delight.

Wisdom in the Wreckage

When life's a wreck, I grab my snack,
Munching on chips while planning my hack.
The vacuum screams that it needs a dance,
As dirt and crumbs leap—a floor's romance.

My to-do list, oh what a mess,
A jumbled jumble of pure distress.
Yet here I am, in the thick of things,
Discovering joy that chaos brings.

Laughter lingers beneath the spills,
With every tumble, the heart just thrills.
A mishap here, a giggle there,
Life's wreckage leads to moments rare.

From broken dishes, wisdom's born,
In tangled tapes, bright ideas are shorn.
So cheers to chaos, our friend on the floor,
Where lessons hide in the humor galore.

Fractals of Life's Canvas

Paint splatters on my canvas bright,
A masterpiece formed from pure delight.
Brush strokes wobble, colors collide,
Creating chaos where dreams can hide.

I trip on my dreams, take a tumble,
Collecting fragments, watch them rumble.
Out of disorder, patterns arise,
With laughter, I plot my wild surprise.

Coffee spills overlap my blue,
A watercolor wonder born anew.
In chaos' grip, I break the mold,
Leaving behind the timid and cold.

Through this mess, joy finds a way,
Fractals of laughter lead the play.
For life's wild patterns, oh so divine,
Remind us all to embrace the design.

Navigating Life's Rough Waters

With a paddle and donut, I sail astray,
The lake's a circus, I'm just here for play.
A fish jumps high, flops down with grace,
Splashing my snacks, it's a slippery race.

Waves toss and turn, I dance with glee,
A duck quacks loudly, it's judging me.
The canoe is laughing, I'm soaked to the bone,
But laughter echoes, I'm never alone.

Life's currents swirl like a funky beat,
I dive through the chaos, ain't it sweet?
For every capsized moment I face,
Is but a reminder, chaos is grace.

So here's to the waters, the laughter it brings,
Amidst all the chaos, my heart gently sings.
With a twist and a turn, I immerse in the fun,
Finding joy as I splash in the sun.

Blossoms of Hope in the Downpour

Raindrops tap dance on my head,
While rubber ducks swim instead.
Puddles form a giant pool,
Where I splash like a silly fool.

Umbrellas flip and take to flight,
As fashion shows become a fright.
Caught between the sun and rain,
I'll dance here, happy with my gain.

Each droplet sparkles like a star,
I'll pretend I'm on a safari tour.
Chasing through the streets I glide,
With a grin I cannot hide.

So here I twirl in silly glee,
In the chaos, I feel so free.
Who knew wet socks could inspire?
In the downpour, my heart's on fire!

The Art of Embracing the Unknown

Lost in the maze of where to go,
Should I bake bread or develop a show?
With every clue a riddle unfurls,
Like tangled hair with a million swirls.

Pick a route or just play pretend,
Living life like it's a blend.
Wearing socks that never match,
Who knows what joy they might hatch?

Oh, here comes the unexpected twist,
As I add sprinkles to my fist.
Cupcakes baking need a partner,
Let's all eat — a sugar starter!

Jump and wiggle, embrace the plight,
In every chaos, there's pure delight.
With laughter echoing through the night,
I'll dance with shadows, what a sight!

Rising from the Ashen Mist

From gray to glow, the tales unfold,
Like burnt toast still daring to be bold.
I rise from ashes, feathered hair,
With chocolate smudges everywhere.

Crumbs collected in a line,
Leading me to donuts divine.
Who knew chaos could lead to this?
Sweet victory, oh what bliss!

Smoke alarms blaring, it's a treat,
Dinner's a war, but I'm on my feet.
With laughter we cook, we burn, we yearn,
Through the madness, still we learn.

So let the fog roll in and crash,
Life's too short to make a splash.
I'll take a bite from the misty dark,
In the chaos, I'll leave my mark!

Constellations Born of Chaos

Stars collide in a cosmic whirl,
My socks are gone, but my cat gives a twirl.
Galaxies dance, and I trip in delight,
Chasing comets all through the night.

With every stumble, a story's spun,
In night's embrace, I have such fun.
Pillow forts and pillow fights,
In this cosmos, joy ignites.

Maps unraveled, lost in the flow,
Navigating life with giggles aglow.
Confetti storms and paper planes,
In chaos, happiness reigns.

So here's to the mess, the tangled crest,
In glorious chaos, I feel so blessed.
Through every fall and unplanned chase,
I find my joy in this wild space!

When Tumult Yields Treasure

In a world where squirrels rule the street,
I trip on my shoelace while dancing to beat.
A sudden wind blows my hat to a tree,
I scream at the sky, "Set my fashion sense free!"

Loud honks and sirens, a symphony play,
But laughter escapes in the strangest of ways.
My neighbor mows grass in a top hat and tie,
Is he dreaming of winning the lawnmower prize?

Bouncing around like a rubber ball,
I join in the nonsense, I'm having a ball!
Each mishap and giggle, a reason to cheer,
In chaos like this, it's so clear that I'm here!

So bring on the madness, let carpets fly high,
With spatulas twirling, we'll all reach for the sky.
When life throws confetti, we'll dance and embrace,
For treasure shines bright in this wild, wacky space.

Finding Voice in the Silence

In the morning so still, my toast starts to cry,
The dog's in a chorus, a soulful goodbye.
But I hum a tune, all whimsical and bright,
As I drown out the chaos with jelly and spite!

Quiet can shout like a giggling fool,
While plants have opinions on who is the coolest.
I talk to my shoes, they always reply,
With a lace and a sparkle, they float to the sky!

The pause in the noise can be tricky, oh dear,
Like socks that get lost in a laundry career.
A bump and a tumble can spark a new song,
In echoes of wild thoughts, where I truly belong.

So let silence dance, with a wiggle and cheer,
The universe chuckles, "Now, come join my sphere!"
Finding my voice in the hush of our space,
Is like ordering ice cream at a knitting race.

The Dance of Unpredictable Moments

A cat on a skateboard whizzes right past,
While I drop my ice cream, oh, what a cast!
With sprinkles and giggles, they stick to my nose,
I waltz through the chaos, it's how the day goes!

The bus takes a detour through puddles and rain,
With each splash we burst like a glittering train.
A banana peels out, makes a bold debut,
And we're rolling and laughing, the funniest crew!

When life takes a turn, like a twist of a fate,
I moonwalk with ducks, that's just how I skate.
Through tumbles and spirals, I leap and I spin,
In this crazy, bizarre waltz, I just gotta grin!

So let's sway to the rhythm of foolish delight,
With dance parties starting at the best types of night.
In moments unpredictable, I find my own beat,
Where each slip and trip makes life oh so sweet!

Radiance from Ruin

A plate hits the ground, a shatter, a splash,
My dinner's now art—what a glorious crash!
With forks flying high and a pasta ballet,
I giggle and wonder if chaos can stay.

My plants wiggle wildly, they assume I can sing,
While I stage dive into the fridge, finding bling.
A leftover pizza performs in style,
And a dance-off with broccoli makes me smile!

In the mess of the moment, the laughter reflects,
That sometimes it's ruin that leads to respect.
For beauty's not perfect, oh not even close,
Like the cat with the bow tie performing a post!

So bring on the blunders, the twists and the bends,
I'll shine through the laughter, my chaos transcends.
In the wreckage of life, we find colors anew,
Radiant and quirky, as we dance through the goo!

www.ingramcontent.com/pod-product-compliance
Lightning Source LLC
Chambersburg PA
CBHW051639160426
43209CB00004B/711